THIS BOOK BELONGS TO:

_____

DISCLAIMER

This book is intended for adults only. It contains fictional illustrations involving crime and dark humor, created purely for entertainment and artistic expression. It does not promote or encourage real-life illegal or harmful behavior. Not suitable for children. Reader discretion is advised.

All rights reserved. No part of this book, including text and illustrations, may be copied, shared, or reproduced in any form without written permission from the publisher. This book is for personal use only. Unauthorized use is a violation of copyright law.

Creating this coloring book has been a joy, and it comes to life through your creativity. Your colors and imagination give each page new meaning. We're truly grateful for the way you bring our work to life.

Your feedback helps others find this book and supports future projects. Thank you for taking a moment to leave a review on Amazon.

With heartfelt appreciation,
Olivia Maren
May 18, 2025

To keep our books affordable and accessible, we use standard paper. For best results with markers, please place a thicker sheet behind the page you're coloring to prevent bleed-through. Thank you for understanding !

Made in United States
North Haven, CT
06 October 2025